ELECTRICIAN

David Overcamp

Children's Press®
A Division of Scholastic Inc.
New York / Toronto / London / Auckland / Sydney
Mexico City / New Delhi / Hong Kong
Danbury, Connecticut

Book Design: Christopher Logan and Daniel Hosek

Photo Credits: Cover © Digital Vision; p. 4 © Reuters NewMedia Inc./Corbis; p. 7 © AP/Wide World Photos; p. 8 © Bettman/Corbis; p. 11 U.S. Department of the Interior National Park Service, Edison National Historic Site; p. 15, 25 © Roger Ressmeyer/Corbis; pp. 18, 21, 31, 33 © Corbis; p. 26 © Roger Ball/Corbis; p. 28 © Jose Luis Pelaez, Inc./Corbis; p. 34 © Getty Images; p. 36 © AFP/Corbis; pp. 40–41 © Craig Aurness/Corbis

Library of Congress Cataloging-in-Publication Data

Overcamp, David.
    Electrician / David Overcamp.
    p. cm.—(Great jobs)
    Summary: Discusses some of the jobs done by electricians, the training and tools needed, and opportunities in the field.
    ISBN 0-516-24086-2 (lib. bdg.)—ISBN 0-516-25924-5 (pbk.)
    1. Electric engineering—Vocational guidance—Juvenile literature.
    2.Electricians—Job descriptions—Juvenile literature. [1.
    Electricians. 2. Vocational guidance.] I. Title. II. Series.

TK159.O94 2003
621.319'24'023—dc21

                                    2003010306

Contents

Introduction   5

1   The Path of Power   9

2   Tasks, Tools, and Training   19

3   Wire to Wire   29

4   Current Thinking   37

New Words   42

For Further Reading   44

Resources   45

Index   47

About the Author   48

Introduction

A summer thunderstorm rolls into town around 11:15 P.M. Inside houses, families watch the weather report on television. They want to see how much damage the storm might cause. A nearby hospital is busy. The hospital is filled with machines that supply life-giving oxygen to patients. Other machines help to pump the patients' blood.

At 11:20, a lightning bolt strikes a special pole on the street. On top of this pole is a transformer. The lightning's surge of electricity fries the transformer. The entire street plunges into darkness. Televisions go blank. Air-conditioning machines are suddenly quiet. Most of the town is affected by the blackout—including the hospital.

Electricians spring into action. A hospital electrician sees that the battery backup system is working.

A single storm such as Hurricane Lili, which struck Louisiana in 2002, can leave thousands of homes without electricity.

She starts up a gas generator on the roof for extra power. Now the hospital's patients won't be in any danger due to the power failure.

Meanwhile, on the street, linemen are also hard at work. A special truck lifts them to the top of the pole. They put a new transformer in place on the pole. With the rain pouring, it's a tough, dangerous job. By midnight, the lights in the neighborhood are back on. Some people have slept right through the storm. They never knew that there was a blackout. If the blackout had continued through the morning, though, things could have gotten messy. Walking outdoors without traffic signals would have been dangerous. Refrigerated foods in homes and grocery stores would have spoiled.

Electricity's power is very useful. Used the wrong way, though, it can also be dangerous. Electricians are skilled men and women who know how to use electricity in the right way. In this book, we will see how electricians set up and run the systems that power our world.

Blizzards and ice storms may force most people indoors. Electricians, however, are expected to restore power to any broken lines.

CHAPTER ONE

The Path of Power

Early Pioneers of Power

Hundreds of years ago, people had little knowledge of the world of electricity. They marveled at lightning in the sky. Yet they didn't know where the bolts of lightning came from. They knew they could get a shock if they walked on carpets and then touched a piece of metal. Yet they didn't really know what static electricity was. It took years of tests to understand how electricity worked.

In June 1752, Benjamin Franklin performed an important test. Franklin flew a kite in a thunderstorm. He attached a metal key to the kite string. When lightning struck the kite, electricity traveled down the string toward the key, causing a brief spark. This helped prove how electricity travels.

Benjamin Franklin's experiment taught the world valuable lessons. After Franklin's success, more people became interested in harnessing electricity's awesome power.

Suddenly, there was a great demand for electricity. Ways to produce large amounts of it were invented. Giant electricity-producing machines called generators were developed, starting in the 1860s. Coal and gas were burned to power the generators. Power plants with generators were built in major cities across the United States.

Scientists such as Thomas Edison made electricity useful to the whole world. Around 1880, Edison invented the lightbulb. Up until then, people lit their homes with gas lamps and candles. Edison's safer, brighter invention appealed to everyone.

Electricity began flowing into people's homes. Items such as irons and heaters became common sights in many households. Factories began to put this energy to work, too. Machines that ran on electricity were invented to help businesses, such as factories, work more quickly.

Today, telephones, radios, and computers use electricity to help people talk to one another. People also began to rely on this type of power to provide entertainment. Without electricity, there would be no television, VCRs, or DVD players.

In Edison's time, owning a home powered by lightbulbs such as this one was considered a luxury.

Power Trip

Electricity follows a path that starts from giant power plants. The path continues through wires into homes and businesses. First, generators at the power plant transform energy into electricity. The energy usually comes from burning different kinds of fuel.

Electricians who work at power plants are called powerhouse electricians. They install and repair cables. These cables connect the generators to step-up transformers.

Most electricity comes from burning coal, oil, or gas, or through using nuclear energy. Each source has its problems. One of the problems is that these energy sources can only be used one time. They also produce waste, such as exhaust. A search is on for cleaner, safer ways to get power. Many people are turning to nature for answers. Several energy sources found in nature are renewable. This means they can be used over and over. Hydropower is one great source of renewable electricity. The force of rushing water generates hydropower. Sunlight and wind can also be used to generate electricity. Electricity can even be produced from the intense heat found in magma. Magma is liquid rock found deep beneath the soil.

Step-up transformers increase the voltage of the electricity. Voltage is how the strength of an electric current is measured. The more volts in a current, the more powerful it is.

In some ways, voltage is similar to water pressure in a garden hose. High water pressure makes the stream out of the hose shoot a great distance. High voltage makes electricity travel long distances, too. The electricity made by a generator is about 25,000 volts. Step-up transformers pump this voltage up. Once it goes through a step-up transformer, the electricity may reach 500,000 volts. This is a very powerful—and dangerous—amount.

Power Lines

After electricity leaves the power plant, it continues on its path. It travels along power lines. Power lines are also called outside lines.

—• TAKING CARE OF BUSINESS

The lines that come into your home are usually either 120 or 220 volts. The batteries that power most cars use only 12 volts.

Powerhouse electricians work with giant transformers like these on a daily basis.

Lineworkers connect the power lines from power plants to homes and businesses. First, they put up utility poles and towers. Then they string power lines between the poles and towers. They also run underground cable in trenches. Each line they build is a new path that the electricity can follow.

Lineworkers face serious dangers when they work. Sometimes lineworkers work with live lines. Live lines have high voltage electricity running through them. They also have to perform precise tasks at great heights. They're often lifted up from a truck inside special baskets. These baskets are insulated. This means they're made of material that protects the workers from being harmed by electricity. Insulated material reduces the danger of electrocution. Lineworkers often must work during storms or tornadoes. Some lineworkers must repair live electric lines while driving rain pours down around them. Of course, water and electricity can be a terrifying combination.

Before electricity gets to your house, its voltage needs to be lowered. Step-down transformers reduce the force of the electricity. They may cut those 500,000 volts down to less than 500.

Throughout the United States, about 100,000 line installers and repairers work on electric lines. Most linepersons make between $17 and $26 an hour. Some make more than $30 an hour.

Inside Wires

Of course, electricity's path doesn't stop at the local utility pole. It continues into homes and businesses. From there, inside electricians take over.

About 700,000 men and women in the United States work as inside electricians. Two-thirds of inside electricians work in construction. Construction electricians install the equipment, appliances, and wires that power buildings. Each building has an electrical panel. All electric circuits run outward from this panel. A circuit is the complete path that an electrical current makes. The electrical panel is like the power plant of the building. Construction electricians install circuit breakers in the panel. Circuit breakers switch the electricity off when too much electrical current is in the system. This is very important. If a circuit contains too much electrical current and shorts out, or overloads, it can cause a fire. It could even cause someone to be electrocuted. Circuit breakers protect against this.

Construction electricians install lights and outlets on the other end of the circuit. They also install everything from smoke alarms to heating and cooling systems. They test what they've installed to make sure it all works properly.

The other group of inside electricians works in maintenance. Big companies that use a lot of power may keep a maintenance electrician on duty 24 hours a day. They try to spot problems before they arise. If any piece of equipment fails, they figure out what the problem is. They repair old or broken circuits. They replace faulty machinery.

Maintenance electricians clean or make minor repairs on equipment on a regular basis. This attention to detail prevents larger or more dangerous problems from happening in the future.

TAKING CARE OF BUSINESS

Construction electricians are the best-paid construction workers. They make more than $32 an hour.

DRESSING
ROOM SIZE 5'x9'-4"
CEILING 9'/DRYWALL
FLOOR: CARPET & PAD

BATH
ROOM SIZE: 5'x6'-6"
CEILING: 9'/DRYWALL
FLOOR: SHEET VINYL

5' C.I. TUB
W/ SHOWER
& ENCLOSURE

CHAPTER TWO

Tasks, Tools, and Training

Electricians need to build their skills in order to tackle the widest range of jobs possible. Whether they're wiring the smallest house or the largest factory, skilled electricians can work almost anywhere. They have to be able to see each job through from start to finish.

Construction electricians often prepare for a job by reading blueprints. These drawings tell them the location of circuits. They explain the wiring system of the building they'll be working on. Studying blueprints also helps construction electricians decide what equipment and tools they'll need for the job.

Next, they arrive at the job site, carrying heavy reels of rolled-up wire. Once inside the building, they drill holes in the walls for conduit. A conduit

To be a successful electrician, it helps to be skilled at subjects such as math and science.

19

is a metal or plastic pipe that contains electrical wires. A conduit protects the wires from wear and tear. The electricians pull wires through the conduit. They install outlets and lights. They also install switches and dimmers. These allow people to control the presence and intensity of the lights.

The job isn't finished until each item is carefully tested. Details have to be checked several times. Every job ends with a visit from the electrical inspector.

The Tools It Takes

Electricians use a variety of hand tools. These include screwdrivers, hammers, and wrenches. Depending on the job, electricians may also use knives, chisels, and pliers.

One special tool that electricians use is called a circuit tester. Circuit testers measure many qualities of electricity. For instance, they measure the presence of electricity. They also measure voltage. Construction and maintenance electricians use power tools, such as saws and drills. They work with

People who work with electricity become familiar with a great number of unusual tools. When electricians read this tool, called a voltmeter, they're able to measure the voltage of electricity.

tools designed to help quickly pull a cable through a conduit.

Line installers often use big machinery. They have to set utility poles using cranes and hoists. Electricians who work on high-voltage wires have to take extreme care. They may use remote-control robots to help them with their tasks. Line repairers sometimes travel in helicopters. This form of travel provides a bird's-eye view of the system of wires they'll need to fix.

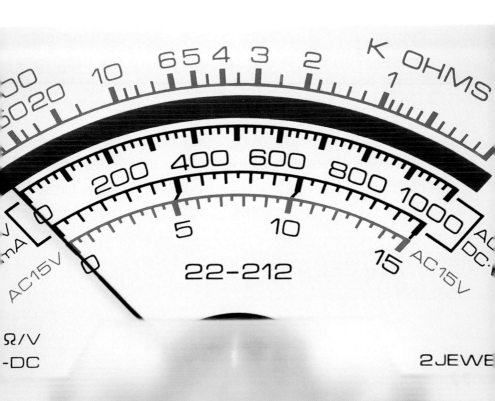

Requirements

Electricians need to keep a clear head at all times. Because of this, drug testing is common. Electricians also need to have some measure of strength and stamina. They may need to lift items weighing 65 pounds (29 kilograms) or more during one job. Another job may require climbing a pole that's over 100 feet (30 meters) high.

Electricians need to be at least eighteen years old. They should have a high school education. They need to take at least one year of algebra. Taking courses in math, shop, physics, and drafting helps provide future electricians with early training.

Electricians' actions must be focused. Sloppy electrical work is dangerous. This is especially true when lineworkers work with live lines. Working with live lines can help prevent power outages. Of course, it also makes for a more dangerous task. In these cases, electricians must use long tools called

FUN FACTS

Because electricians tell wires apart by color, they cannot be color-blind.

hot sticks. Hot sticks protect them from electrical currents. The workers must be sure that they're using insulated tools and wearing insulated gloves. Failure to do so could cause personal harm—even death.

• TAKING CARE OF BUSINESS

If line repairs cannot be made safely, electricians may cause a planned power outage.

Apprentice Training

Most electricians start out as apprentices. It's the surest path to starting a successful career. Apprentices train on the job for three or four years. This may translate into 8,000 hours of training!

During the day, apprentices work with skilled electricians. At night, they take classes to learn how electricity works. They're taught how to read blueprints. They also learn about the National Electrical Code. This code is a set of rules having to do with electrical work. It serves as an electrician's guide for wiring.

Those who want to become apprentices take tests. These tests measure important abilities, such as math, reading, and motor skills. An applicant's ability to learn and make sense of details is also tested. All applicants are rated after completing all these tests. They then must wait for an apprenticeship opening. This wait may take months, even years.

A joint program of the National Electrical Contractors Association (NECA) and the International Brotherhood of Electrical Workers (IBEW) trains many apprentices. The IBEW is the largest union for electricians. Like other unions, the IBEW tries to get its members the best pay and working conditions. Another group called the Independent Electrical Contractors (IEC), also offers early electrical training.

There are many trade schools available for beginning electricians as well. Some programs even allow you to take courses from home.

Electricians can't afford to do sloppy work on their projects. It's important that apprentices receive guidelines and instructions each step of the way.

Higher Levels

Skilled electricians may take an exam to get a license. This license serves as evidence that an electrician knows his or her craft well. Most licensed electricians are at the journeyworker level. This means they are professionals who can supervise other workers. However, they continue learning and training over the course of their entire careers.

Some journeyworkers will later become electrical contractors. About 10 percent of electricians are self-employed as contractors. Contractors own their own businesses. They are responsible for their own success.

Many jobs only help or affect a few people. During a power outage, however, a whole town might depend on a lineman like the one shown here.

CHAPTER THREE

Wire to Wire

Antonio wakes at the crack of dawn, eager to start his day. He is an apprentice electrician. He is just getting started on 2,000 hours of residential electrical training. He'll learn more and more about how to wire and bring power to homes and apartments. This is his first week working with Lisa, a journeyworker electrician. The same electrical contractor has employed Lisa for three years.

Yesterday, Antonio finished his first small job. He and Lisa wired a new kitchen in an old house. Antonio was surprised by the amount of equipment they used on the job. They used huge spools of insulated, multi-colored wire. Some of the wires were aluminum. Most of them, however, were made of copper. Lisa and Antonio packed a lot of steel electrical boxes. They filled these boxes with wires

Journeyworker electricians must oversee the work done by apprentices.

based on an electrical plan. They also packed junction boxes. Junction boxes are an electrical version of a railway station. In a station, trains arrive and depart at different tracks, going off in many directions. In a junction box, conduit feeds in and out of the box, leading electrical currents to and from different destinations.

A Tougher Task

Today, Lisa and Antonio are wiring a new house. This will be a bigger job than the one they tackled yesterday. It could be a more difficult job, too.

Antonio meets Lisa at the electrical contractor's shop at 7:30 A.M. They arrive at the house thirty minutes later. The two of them notice that the carpenters have finished framing the house. This means that all the boards are in place. The roof and the walls have not been assembled yet. Because of this, the place looks like a skeleton of a completed house.

Lisa and Antonio study the blueprints. Lisa points out the location of the service panel. They're supposed to install it on a wall next to the kitchen.

When electricians encounter a problem during their work day, they always discuss the situation together.

The kitchen is on the first floor. The wires from the utility pole will enter the house at the service panel.

Antonio and Lisa carry the service panel from their van to the house. Once they walk beside the kitchen area, they spot a big problem. There's a doorway where a wall should be! Antonio takes out the blueprints and double checks them. He traces over the blueprint with his finger.

"Am I making a mistake?" Antonio asks.

Lisa glances at the blueprints and shakes her head. "No, you're right. Something has changed."

She calls the house's general contractor, Peter. Peter works directly for the homeowner. Peter is the person who hired Lisa's electrical contractor to handle the wiring. He explains to Lisa that the homeowner recently made a surprise change. Last week, this homeowner decided to put a closet next to the kitchen. "I forgot to tell you about his change," Peter says, apologizing.

Antonio looks worried. He isn't sure how they'll be able to correct the problem. Lisa hangs up the phone. She assures Antonio that they'll figure something out. Lisa thinks it may be possible to install the service panel in the laundry room. The laundry room is in the basement directly underneath the kitchen.

Since the house doesn't have stairways yet, Antonio and Lisa must use a ladder. They climb down to the basement. The basement has a concrete slab floor. Lisa carefully looks over a copy of the electrical specification for the house. The specification is a list. It tells exactly what Lisa's company

Electricians have to remember and process a lot of information during each job. That's why having a blueprint always makes a tough project a little easier.

has agreed to provide. The laundry room has a special outlet on the specification. The dryer uses more electricity than most appliances. Most of the outlets supply 120 volts. The dryer outlet is 220 volts. It takes a special plug.

Lisa decides there's enough room for the panel to fit in the basement. Antonio goes back upstairs and hands the panel down to Lisa. The two of them bolt the panel into place. Lisa tells Antonio they should work on separate tasks for awhile.

Lisa installs outlet boxes on the first floor. Antonio works in the basement, drilling holes in the boards above him. After he's done, they'll run conduit through these holes from the basement to the first floor. Every so often, Lisa monitors Antonio's work. "You're doing fine," she says, inspecting the holes. "Just remember to stay focused. Don't rush, or you'll do a sloppy job."

By noon, Antonio finished drilling all the holes. He and Lisa drive to a restaurant. They discuss the job over a well-earned lunch. They've lost some time this morning because of the service panel's location change. Lisa is sure they'll be able to make up that time, though. After lunch, they bend the conduit. Then they run it from the basement to the first floor. Antonio concentrates hard to get the measurements exactly right. He likes the way the conduit fits together like a giant puzzle. At 4:30 p.m., they call it a day. They clean up their tools and the extra conduit. Tomorrow, they'll finish bending the last few pieces. This house will soon come to life, with working electricity.

Electricians must always check to make sure that they have done their work properly. Here, an electrician tests an outlet box that has just been installed.

CHAPTER FOUR

Current Thinking

Many journeyworkers look forward to owning their own businesses. Other electricians choose to go down different career paths. This book has shown you some of those paths.

Many other options are available. Some electricians travel across the world. Others get the chance to rub elbows with celebrities and see their work come to life on the silver screen. This chapter shows you the more unusual roles electricians fulfill.

Marine Electricians

Marine electricians often do most of their work on ships and barges. These vessels have large, complex electrical systems. Motors on many ships are powered by onboard generators. Electricity helps a crew communicate with one another, as well as with

The gaffers who provide electricity on movie sets are often under a great deal of pressure. Their light kits have to be up and running the instant the director is ready to start filming a scene.

other ships. Marine electricians help keep sonar and radar systems up and running. It's also important that they carefully maintain these complex wiring systems. If the power on a ship shorts out, its crew could find themselves lost at sea.

Many marine electricians get their training in the navy. They learn how to use a wide number of hand and power tools. They may continue to work on military vessels for years. Others might wind up working for shipping companies that transport goods across the open seas.

Film Electricians

Film electricians work on movies and television shows. They are often called gaffers. Gaffers set up huge light fixtures on the sets and sound stages. Gaffers use lighting to create special effects. TV and film directors also rely on gaffers to enhance a film's mood. Lighting can make a film seem cheerful, mysterious, or even frightening.

Sometimes, the movies are filmed in locations that don't have too many outlets. Because of this,

FUN FACTS

The word gaffer is the British slang term for grandfather. It is used as a term of respect.

gaffers often have to transport portable generators and transformers.

Movie lights often gobble huge amounts of electricity. Gaffers get used to running large cables everywhere to power all the lights. They have to make sure that all the cables and cords don't get in the crew's way.

Gaffers get used to working long hours on the set. They get used to tense, high-pressure situations. However, they get to see their favorite movie stars at work. They also get to see their names rolling in the film or show's credits!

Future Opportunities

In the Internet age, electricity has become more important than ever. The lighting in houses and offices has become more complex. More and more often, a central computer controls the levels of light and heat in a building. Electricians must adapt to new ways of doing things.

In the future, we may learn how to develop new sources of energy. Electricity may be supplied in exciting new ways. However, the demand for electricity won't stop. In fact, it's very likely that the demand will grow even higher. Skilled, hardworking electricians will be needed to meet these demands for power. They'll have to complete the circuits from generator to outlet. They'll be trusted to keep each machine and wire running smoothly. Those men and women who can supply power to the people have a glowing future ahead of them.

apprentice (uh-**pren**-tiss) someone who learns a trade or craft by working with a skilled person

blueprint (**bloo**-print) a detailed plan for a project

cable (**kay**-buhl) a tight bundle of wires used for carrying electricity

circuit (**sur**-kit) the complete path that an electrical current can flow around

circuit breaker (**sur**-kit **bray**-kur) a device that switches the electricity off when there is too much current in an electrical system

conduit (**kon**-doo-it) a plastic or metal pipe that protects electric wires

contractor (**kon**-trakt-ur) a person or company that does construction jobs for a set amount of money

generator (**jen**-uh-ray-tur) a machine that produces electricity by turning a magnet inside a coil of wire

hydropower (**hye**-druh-pou-ur) electricity made from energy produced by running water

insulation (**in**-suh-lay-shun) material used by electricians that keeps electricity from harming them

journeyworker (**jur**-nee-wurk-ur) a skilled worker who has passed a licensing exam

lineworkers (**line**-wurk-urz) electricians who install the lines that travel from power plants to homes and businesses

power lines (**pou**-ur **linez**) the wires that carry electricity from the power plant to buildings; also called outside lines

step-down transformer (**step-doun** transs-**for**-mur) a device that lowers the voltage of electricity

step-up transformer (**step-up** transs-**for**-mur) a device that raises the voltage of electricity

voltage (**vohl**-tij) the force of electricity

wire (**wire**) a long, thin, flexible piece of metal; can be used to conduct an electrical current

FOR FURTHER READING

Donnelley, Karen J. *Electrician*. Mankato, MN: Capstone Press, 2001.

Lytle, Elizabeth Stewart. *Careers as an Electrician*. New York: Rosen Publishing Group, 1999.

Parker, Steve. *Electricity*. New York: Dorling Kindersley, 2000.

Organizations

Independent Electrical Contractors
4401 Ford Avenue, Suite 1100
Alexandria, VA 22302
Phone: (703) 549-7351
Fax: (703) 549-7448
E-mail: info@ieci.org

International Brotherhood of Electrical Workers
1125 15th Street N.W.
Washington, DC 20005
Phone: (202) 833-7000
Fax: (202) 467-6316

National Electrical Contractors
3 Bethesda Metro Center, Suite 1100
Bethesda, MD 20814
Phone: (301) 657-3110
Fax: (301) 215-4500
E-mail: webmaster@necanet.org

Web Sites

Richmond Power and Light—Learn About Electricity

www.rp-l.com/rplkids.htm

This Web site links you to a great description of how electricity travels from the power plant to people's homes and businesses.

Kidszone—U.S. Department of Energy

*www.energy.gov/engine/
content.do?BT_CODE=KIDS.html*

This Web site provides a portal into learning what roles energy plays in all our lives. It's full of fun facts, milestones, quizzes, and games.

National Joint Apprenticeship and Training Committee

www.njatc.org

The Web site lets you know all about starting an electrician apprenticeship. It lists the types of programs available, and displays some sample test questions. If you're interested in a career in this field, this site will give you a running start.

A
apprentice, 29

B
blackout, 5–6
blueprint, 31

C
cable, 14, 21
circuit, 16, 20
circuit breakers, 16
circuit tester, 20
conduit, 19–21, 30, 35
contractor, 29–30, 32
current, 13, 16

E
Edison, Thomas, 10
electrical panel, 16

F
Franklin, Benjamin, 9

G
gaffers, 38, 39
generator, 6, 13, 41

H
hot sticks, 23

I
Independent Electrical
    Contractors (IEC), 24
International Brotherhood
    of Electrical Workers
    (IBEW), 24

J
journeyworkers, 27, 37
junction box, 30

L
license, 27
lineworkers, 14, 22
live lines, 14, 22

M
maintenance, 17, 20

N

National Electrical Code, 23

National Electrical Contractors Association (NECA), 24

O

outages, 22

P

power, 6, 10, 12–14, 16–17, 20, 22, 29, 38–39, 41

powerhouse electricians, 12

power lines, 13–14

power plants, 10, 12, 14

S

step-down transformers, 15

step-up transformers, 12–13

T

tests, 9, 24

tools, 19–23, 35, 38

trade schools, 24

U

utility poles, 14, 21

V

voltage, 13–15, 20–21

W

wire, 19, 29, 41

About the Author

David Overcamp lives in Brooklyn, New York. He is an electrician and lighting designer for theater and fashion shows. On the side, he wires houses and industrial shops. This is his first book.